How Can I Prepare My Young Child for Reading?

Paula C. Grinnell

Copyright 1984 by the
International Reading Association, Inc.

Library of Congress Cataloging in Publication Data

Grinnell, Paula C.
   How can I prepare my young child for reading?

   (An IRA Micromonograph)
   1. Reading Readiness. 2. Reading (Preschool)
3. Domestic education. 4. Children – Books and reading.
I. Title. II. Series.
LB1140.5.R4C74 1984   372.4'1   83-12969
ISBN 0-87207-881-7

Photo credits: Mary Loewenstein-Anderson, pages 5, 10

How Can I Prepare My Young Child for Reading?

As your child's first and most important teacher, you need to know how children learn to read. When does preparation for reading begin? What can you, as a parent, do to prepare your child for reading? The answers to these questions will affect your child's learning throughout life. So much development takes place before first grade that your child's elementary school teachers can only supplement what you have already done.

This pamphlet deals with the critical years from birth through kindergarten. Read on to find out how you can help your child become a reader.

When Does Preparation for Reading Begin?

Are you surprised that the answer is "from birth"? As a parent of an infant, this is the best time for you to learn how to assist your child's development. Infants are able to learn more than people think. Shortly after birth, infants can turn their heads toward sounds and can look at objects and people. Your infant starts learning immediately, and this learning contributes to readiness to read. Here are some specific ways that you can help prepare your young child for reading.

Talk to Your Child

It is essential that you talk to and listen to your child wherever and whenever you can. The more you talk with your child, the more your child will learn and will want to talk to you. This is the first major step toward reading.

Young children usually do not talk the same way adults talk. They pronounce words differently, confuse some words (like he, she, her, him), put words in different sentence order, and use verb tenses in an unusual manner. When your child does these things, teach the youngster how to speak by repeating the word, phrase, or sentence in the correct way. Be positive. Saying "That's wrong" or "Can't you say it right?" will discourage your child from trying.

Just as your child develops from wiggling to turning over to crawling to walking to jumping, and so on, your child also develops from babbling to talking. Generally, when children are ready to walk, they walk; and when children are ready to speak like adults, they do.

Both reading and talking are forms of communication. The knowledge of spoken language that children develop forms the basis for their knowledge of written language. Thus, knowing how to communicate ideas by speaking and listening will help your child learn how to communicate ideas by writing and reading. Here are some suggestions for talking to your infant.

▶ While feeding your infant, talk about the food.

▶ While dressing your infant, talk about what you are doing. "Now I'm going to put on your shirt. Help me by pushing your hand through the sleeve."

▶ While bathing your baby, make noises the infant can imitate.

▶ While riding in the car, talk about the scenery or where you are going. Sing a song or nursery rhyme.

As your child gets older, you will want to talk with and listen to the youngster in more mature ways. Here are

Exploring books can be a real adventure for young children.

some examples of ways in which you can draw your child into conversation.

▶ While grocery shopping, talk with your child about what foods you're buying, why you're buying them, how much they cost, and when you plan to serve them. Ask what foods your child would like you to buy.

▶ Before making a meal, discuss what your child likes to eat and how to prepare it.

▶ Before bedtime, make up a story together. You can start the story, let your child continue it for a sentence or two, and then take your turn again. Be sure to create an ending.

▶ Before taking a trip, talk with your child about where you're going, what you'll see, what you'll do. If you're going to the zoo, talk about the animals you might see, look them up in the encyclopedia, and draw pictures of them. While you're at the zoo, talk about the things you see and compare them with what you expected to see. After your trip, talk about what you saw, what you liked, and what you want to see the next time.

These kinds of activities should be continued through the elementary school. When your child becomes four, five, or six years old, you can add activities like those that follow.

▶ Set aside one night a week for family games. Use games appropriate for your child, such as Memory, Candy Land, or Chutes and Ladders.

▶ When taking a car trip, adapt games to meet your child's knowledge and interest levels. Play Twenty Questions, I Spy, The Alphabet Game, or The Number Game.

▶ When playing Twenty Questions, one person thinks of something and tells the other players whether it is an animal, an animal product, a vegetable, a vegetable product, or a mineral. Items such as steak, hamburger, beef stew, potato salad, carrot soup, and guacamole dip are legitimate because they are products derived from animals or vegetables. Once an item is decided upon, the other players try to guess it by taking turns asking questions that can be answered with yes, no, sometimes, or I don't know. Initially, players should strive to ask questions that will give them information about the categories into which the item could fit. For example, "Is it bigger than my teddy bear? Can you eat it? Can it move by itself?" Officially, the game should stop after twenty questions if no one has guessed correctly. If the players agree, however, the game could be extended. The person to decide on the next item can be chosen based on who guessed the correct answer, or everyone can take a turn.

▶ When playing I Spy, one person thinks of an object in a car that can be seen by everyone. If the object is a blouse, the person can say, "I spy with my little eye something beginning with B," or "...something yellow," or "...something to wear." Parents can focus on letters, colors, or categories depending on their child. The other players attempt to figure out what the person spied by guessing objects in the car, and their guesses are answered with a simple yes or no. When the object is finally guessed, the person who got the correct answer gets the privilege of "spying" the next object.

▶ When playing The Alphabet Game, each player tries to find the letters, in sequential order, on signs that can be seen from the car. Begin by looking for an A. You may find a Watch Out for Children sign. Since there is an A in the sign, you now should look for B. The license plate in front of you may read CBZ 693. That would give you B and C, so that next you begin looking for D. This game can be played as a group effort with younger children, with partners, or in individual competition.

▶ When playing The Number Game, follow the same procedures as you did for The Alphabet Game. The game is over when a player has found all the numbers between 1 and 10 in sequential order.

Read to Your Child

Read to your child every day, gradually increasing the amount of time until you are reading about fifteen minutes a day to your four or five year old. Even infants enjoy hearing nursery rhymes and listening to their parents name familiar objects in books. Toddlers like books with simply written stories. Slightly older children like all kinds of books: poetry, fairy tales, folktales, humorous, fanciful, and factual stories.

Some families like to have reading time just before nap or bedtime. Others prefer more spontaneous reading. Find the method that is best for your family, and read, read, read. Just as children need to hear a lot of spoken language in order to talk, they need to hear a lot of written language in order to read.

Grandparents and children love reading together.

Reading to your child helps build positive attitudes toward reading and exposes your child to a variety of books. You should strive to make the experience so pleasant that you and your child look forward to your special reading times together. As your child gets older, these positive experiences with books will encourage the child to seek out books and other reading materials.

Avoid putting pressure on your child. Do not expect more than the child is capable of giving. Each child develops at a *different* rate and parents should support this pace of growth. If reading experiences become consistently unpleasant, your child will learn to avoid reading in order to get away from the memories of unhappy times associated with reading.

Some ways you can help make reading fun as well as educational for your child follow.

- Know your child's attention span, and don't go beyond it. Some toddlers will sit for hours listening to and looking at books; others can tolerate only a minute or two of quiet time with books. When toddlers have difficulty sitting still, read to them while they are playing. Play recorded nursery rhymes, stories, and songs at bedtime, at playtime, or while riding in the car. Recite nursery rhymes while rocking your child or simply sitting close by.

- Know your child's interests. Some toddlers are interested in hearing fairy tales or stories. Others only want to hear nursery rhymes or books about familiar subjects. Follow your child's lead in choosing books of interest at the moment.

- Talk about the book before, during, and after reading with the emphasis on discussion, avoiding right or wrong answers. With younger children you will naturally lead the discussion by pointing to and talking about the pictures, exchanging opinions, rewording what occurred in the story, and responding to your child's questions and comments. As your child grows, you can discuss the story through whatever thoughts the story stimulates.

- Ask questions about the story when your child is ready to interact in this way. Be positive by accepting all of your child's thoughts and then discussing other possible solutions. Ask questions that do not require "right" answers. The purpose of these questions is to get your child to think about the story and to gain a better understanding of the story and the author's message. You could ask, "What do you think this story will be about? What do you think will happen next? Did you like the way the story ended? How would you like the story to end?"

- Let youngsters read with you when they know a story well enough. At first you might pause so they can supply a word you're certain they will know. Later, they can repeat refrains with you from well-known stories such as *The Gingerbread Man* or *The Three Little Pigs*.

Now that you have some ideas on how to make reading enjoyable, here are some suggestions for fitting reading into a busy schedule.

▶ When you're nursing or giving your baby a bottle, recite some nursery rhymes.

▶ When your baby is fussy, try to quiet the child by reading or singing some rhymes.

▶ When you want a quiet moment together with a child of any age, pick up a book and read.

▶ Before you go to the doctor or dentist, prepare your child by reading a book that shows what the doctor or dentist does.

▶ While waiting in checkout lines, doctors' offices, restaurants, train stations, or airports, have a book on hand for reading and discussing.

▶ Before and/or after watching a television special based on a book, read the book or a similar story to your child.

Reading aloud to children helps stimulate their interest in books.

Let Your Child Read

Children need your approval in their experiences with reading on their own. When children first "read" books, they may simply practice turning the pages. Later, they may practice "reading" a book from the pictures or reciting a story while turning the pages of a book they have memorized. This is all good practice and these reading behaviors should be supported with comments like "You're reading very nicely. Will you read a book to me? I like to listen to you read."

As children get older, they may try reading the words in a book. Allow this time together to become fun. This can be accomplished best by not forcing children to struggle through every word. When a child comes to a word that is not known, rather than ask the child to sound out the word, it is better to simply read the word aloud and then allow the child to continue. The purpose of reading is to understand what is being read, and if too much effort is spent on figuring out how to say each word, the meaning will get lost. The parent's goal is not to teach the child to read; that is the responsibility of the elementary school teacher.

Parents can help most by encouraging in their children a love of and an interest in reading. Some ways you can do this are listed here.

▶ Put brightly colored cloth or cardboard books in your baby's crib or playpen.

▶ Choose books for gifts to children so they can build their own libraries.

▶ Take your three, four, or five year old to the library for special programs like storytime.

▶ Get your three year old a library card and take the child to the library regularly. Encourage your child to choose books to bring home and read alone or with you.

▶ Get books that have cassette tapes or records with them. These are available at the library and are good because your child can spend time alone listening to the story while looking through the book. If you have a cassette and/or record player, your child can listen independently.

▶ Put books in various places in the house where your child can reach them. Then your child can pick up a book and look through it at any time.

▶ Order a magazine subscription for your child.

Let Your Child Write

Your child needs lots of opportunities to practice writing. Have many different kinds of materials to write on and to write with, and keep them in a place where your child can reach them. Paper should be in different sizes, colors, kinds, and textures. Writing implements should include thick and thin markers, pens, pencils, colored pencils, and crayons.

Be patient and enjoy watching your child gain competence in writing. At first children just scribble, then they imitate writing by making straight lines and swirls, then they practice making letters and writing messages with such creative spelling that possibly only the writer can read them. Gradually, however, everyone will understand the child's writing.

Usually, when children are learning how to write and spell, it does not matter whether their spelling is accurate. There are times, however, when it is important that the spelling be correct. For instance, your child would want to spell a friend's name correctly when sending a birthday card. To assist, you could print the name for your child to copy; or you could say one letter at a time, pausing while your child prints it.

Just as listening and speaking develop together, so do reading and writing. Here are some ideas for giving your child opportunities to write.

- ▶ When you make out a shopping list, let your child make out a list, too. A younger child may scribble, and an older one may add items to your list using creative spelling.
- ▶ When you write a letter to someone your child knows, let your child write a message as well, either on your paper or on a separate sheet.
- ▶ When you write checks, give your child paper to write checks on.
- ▶ When a friend or relative has a birthday, suggest that your child make a card.
- ▶ When your own child has a birthday, let your child or an older sibling help write the party invitations.
- ▶ Buy your three, four, or five year old an unlined notebook in which to write or draw daily.

Be a Model

Children need to see their parents reading in a variety of situations, reading different kinds of materials, and reading for different reasons—for pleasure and for specific purposes. Your child should see you reading cookbooks, magazines, newspapers, instructional materials, road signs, maps, and informational books. Your child should see you reading in the home, in the library, and in restaurants. You should tell your child why you are reading these different things and what kinds of information you are learning from these varied sources.

Your child will have a head start on reading if you show that you enjoy reading. Some suggestions for doing this follow.

Children can help one another develop a love of reading.

▶ When your child needs a rest room, read aloud the signs on the doors and help the youngster reach the correct rest room.

▶ When you look for a parking space, talk about the signs. "I can't park here because that sign says No Parking."

▶ When you are assembling a toy, read aloud from the instructions and allow your child to participate.

- After dinner, have a family reading time when everyone reads something together or separately, silently or aloud. Set the rules and the time to fit your family's needs.
- When you read an interesting article or book, tell your child about it.
- When you need some quiet time, tell your child that you want to read. Your youngster can get a book and sit with you or do something else alone for a few minutes while you enjoy your own reading.
- When your child asks a question that you can't answer, say, "Let's look it up together." Use a resource book together at home or take a trip to the library.
- While your child is finding a book at the library, look for one that you would like to read yourself and check it out.

Encourage Your Child's Interest in Reading and Writing

Without meaning to, some parents discourage their children from reading and writing by saying such things as, "You're too little for books. That book is too easy for you. That's not your name; that's just scribbling. You didn't read that book; you just turned the pages." What is meant by reading and writing changes as people grow. Your toddler doesn't walk with the same skill and coordination as an adult, but we still call what the child does "walking." Thus, when children "read" or "write," they believe they are reading or writing.

In addition to complimenting your child's attempts at using written language, you can demonstrate your interest in your youngster's activities. Here are some ways in which you can show your interest.

- ▶ Keep a bulletin board in the kitchen, family room, bedroom, or wherever it is convenient for your family. Display your child's work on it, periodically read what's written, and comment on a particular piece of work.
- ▶ Respond to your child's questions about reading, writing, and spelling.
- ▶ Put magnetic letters on the refrigerator, and let your child play with them. As your child grows older, use the letters to write words or messages to one another.
- ▶ Before giving your child a piece of paper to write on, clearly print the youngster's name in the corner. Eventually, your child will recognize the letters and the name.
- ▶ When your child draws a picture, ask the youngster to tell you about it. Print what the child says on the paper, read it back so the child can listen, and display the written words on the bulletin board. Don't expect your child to read these words back to you. It is sufficient for your child to learn that one's words can be written down. As children grow, they may have more things they want written down. When children are ready, they begin to read some of their own words for themselves.

Above all, show through your own reactions that you value your child and what the child produces. In their own time, children become readers.

Recommended Reading for Parents

Books

A Parent's Guide to Children's Reading, fifth edition. Nancy Larrick. Bantam Books, 1982.

Developing Active Readers: Ideas for Parents, Teachers, and Librarians. Dianne L. Monson and DayAnn K. McClenathan, Editors. International Reading Association, 1979.

Helping Children Read: Ideas for Parents, Teachers, and Librarians. Susan Glazer and Carol Brown, Editors. New Jersey Reading Association, 1980.

On Learning to Read: The Child's Fascination with Meaning. Bruno Bettelheim and Karen Zelan. Knopf, 1982.

Reading Begins at Home, second edition. Marie Clay and Dorothy Butler. Heinemann Educational Books, 1987.

The Beginnings of Writing, second revised edition. Charles A. Temple. Allyn & Bacon, 1988.

The Reading Triangle: Parents Can Help Children Succeed in Reading. Linda M. Clinard. David S. Lake Publishers, 1985.

The World's Best Indoor Games. Gyles Brandreth. Pantheon, 1982.

Magazines

Cricket Magazine. Open Court Publishing, 1058 Eighth Street, LaSalle, IL 61301.

Highlights for Children. 2300 W. Fifth Avenue, P.O. Box 269, Columbus, OH 43216.

Ranger Rick. National Wildlife Federation, 8925 Leesburg Pike, Vienna, VA 22180.

Sesame Street Magazine. P.O. Box 2895, Boulder, CO 80321.

World. National Geographic Society, 17 and M Streets NW, Washington, DC 20036.

Resources for Parents from IRA

Books

Comics to Classics: A Parent's Guide to Books for Teens and Preteens. Arthea (Charlie) Reed. No. 798. US$8.95; IRA members, US$7.95.

The Read-Aloud Handbook, revised edition. Jim Trelease. Published by Penguin Books and codistributed by IRA. No. 633. US$8.95; IRA members, US$8.25.

To order, send your check to: International Reading Association, 800 Barksdale Road, PO Box 8139, Newark, DE 19714-8139, USA. Please specify both title and publication number when ordering.

Parent Booklets

How Can I Prepare My Young Child for Reading? Paula Grinnell. No. 163

You Can Help Your Young Child with Writing. Marcia Baghban. No. 160

Helping Your Child Become a Reader. Nancy Roser. No. 161

You Can Encourage Your High School Student to Read. Jamie Myers. No. 162

Single copies of these parent booklets are available at a cost of US$1.75 each, prepaid only. Send your check to Parent Booklets at the address above. Please specify both title and publication number when ordering.

Parent Brochures

IRA has available ten brochures covering a variety of topics pertaining to ways in which parents can help children of all ages become readers. To receive single copies of all ten brochures, send a self-addressed envelope stamped with first class postage for *three* ounces to Parent Brochures at the address above. The brochures are available in bulk quantities also, and ordering information appears in each brochure. (Requests from outside the USA should include a self-addressed envelope, but postage is not required.)

Children's Choices

Children's Choices is a yearly list of books that children identify as their favorites. To receive a single copy, send a self-addressed envelope stamped with first class postage for *four* ounces to Children's Choices at the address above.

INTERNATIONAL READING ASSOCIATION
OFFICERS 1988-1989
President Patricia S. Koppman; *Vice President* Dale D. Johnson; *Vice President Elect* Carl Braun; *Executive Director* Ronald W. Mitchell

DIRECTORS 1988-1989
Marie C. DiBiasio; Vincent Greaney; Hans U. Grundin; Jerome C. Harste; Jane M. Hornburger; Merrillyn Brooks Kloefkorn; Ann McCallum; Dolores B. Malcolm; Nancy W. Seminoff

The International Reading Association attempts, through its publications, to provide a forum for a wide spectrum of opinions on reading. This policy permits divergent viewpoints without assuming the endorsement of the Association.

This booklet is part of a series designed to provide practical ideas parents can use to help their children become readers. Many of the booklets are being copublished by IRA and the ERIC Clearinghouse on Reading and Communication Skills.

The International Reading Association is
an 80,000 member nonprofit education
organization devoted to the improvement
of reading instruction and the promotion
of the lifetime reading habit.